B2 Writing

Cambridge Masterclass

Margaret Cooze

© Prosperity Education Ltd. 2023

Registered offices: Sherlock Close, Cambridge
CB3 0HP, United Kingdom

First published 2023

ISBN: 978-1-913825-80-5

This publication is in copyright. Subject to statutory exception and to the provisions of relevant collective licensing agreements, no reproduction of any part may take place without the written permission of Prosperity Education.

The moral right of the author has been asserted.

'Cambridge B2 First' and 'FCE' are brands belonging to The Chancellor, Masters and Scholars of the University of Cambridge and are not associated with Prosperity Education or its products.

Designed by ORP Cambridge

For further information and resources, visit:
www.prosperityeducation.net

To infinity and beyond.

Contents

Introduction — 5

Task type 1. **Essay** — 15

Task type 2. **Article** — 23

Task type 3. **Email** — 31

Task type 4. **Letter of application** — 39

Task type 5. **Report** — 47

Task type 6. **Review** — 55

Practice tests — 63

Margaret Cooze holds an MA in Applied Linguistics and an MSc in English Language Teaching Management, and has worked in senior roles at Cambridge English Language Assessment and Cambridge Assessment International Education. She is the author of several ELT resources published by Cambridge University Press.

Introduction

Cambridge B2 First Writing

Welcome to this book on the Cambridge B2 First Writing paper. B2 First is one of the exams in the series provided by Cambridge Assessment – part of the University of Cambridge. It is in the middle of the range of tests they provide in General English:

A2	Key (KET)
B1	Preliminary (PET)
B2	First (FCE)
C1	Advanced (CAE)
C2	Proficiency (CPE)

The references next to each test refer to the CEFR Level (Common European Framework of Reference), and show the language level of each test.

For CEFR B2 Writing, you will be able to:

- communicate your ideas in writing on a range of topics
- write clearly and in some detail
- explain your viewpoint and give advantages and disadvantages
- recognise the reader of texts and use a suitable register
- show a good range of different grammatical structures
- show a good range of suitable vocabulary for the tasks set
- recognise the functional language needed in tasks.

How does the test work?

You can take the B2 First exam on a computer or on paper. The content is the same for both forms of the test. The B2 First Writing papers give you the opportunity to show your language skills. The topics of tasks are chosen so that they are relevant to the typical student taking this exam, so you should find that you have enough ideas to write about. Each question will guide you by identifying the context, the purpose for writing and the target reader. It is important to remember that you aren't being tested on the subject content of the tasks. So, if the topic of the Part 1 question, for example, is education, you aren't expected to be an expert about this topic. The test format is:

Time allowed	1 hour 20 minutes
Number of parts	2
Number of questions	Part 1: one compulsory question Part 2: one optional question from a choice of three
Task types	article, informal email, essay, letter of application, report, review
Length	each answer should be 140–190 words long

Task types

There are six possible task types in the B2 First Writing paper.

Essay

Part 1 (Question 1) of the Writing paper is always an essay written for your teacher, and the start of the question wording is always the same:

> In your English class you have been talking about [topic]. Now, your English teacher has asked you to write an essay.
>
> Write your essay using all the notes and giving reasons for your point of view.

There will be two prompts or points given for you to include in your response, and a third prompt for you to include something based on your own ideas or experience. You must add something for this point. Remember, you don't have to tell the truth! The examiners won't know, so if you don't have experience or an opinion you can make something up.

An essay can be organised in different ways, but it is useful to think of having one idea or focus per paragraph, and a short introduction and conclusion. Essays are written in a semi-formal register as you are writing for your teacher.

Email

You may be asked to write an email in the B2 First Writing paper. Email tasks are informal and are usually written to a friend or someone you study with. The question will tell you what to include in your email, and you will need to make sure that you include everything. Often you will need to include information about yourself in emails or your opinion on something.

Letter of application

This task will be to reply to a notice or advertisement to apply for something. It could be an application for a job or a course, but the question will make this clear. Remember when you write your letter to have a suitable opening and close, for example 'Dear Mrs Linton,' and 'Kind regards…', or something similar.

Article

An article is usually written for an English-language magazine or website. The idea is that the reader will have things in common with you. Imagine a group of your friends reading your article. An article should have some opinion or comment that the reader will be interested in reading. A title is useful to attract attention, and it's good to try to give a strong ending to leave the reader with something to think about.

Report

A report is usually written for a teacher or school principal, or a specific group such as the members of an English club. Reports are factual and have a clear purpose as someone has asked you to write the report. They can include opinions about the topic too. Report questions usually ask you to describe something that has happened, and to make suggestions for changes or recommendations. They are typically quite formal.

Review

A review is usually written for an English-language website or magazine. You will be asked to give your opinion about something or somewhere. The aim of a review is for other people to decide if they want to try what you are reviewing, so you will be describing and recommending something. The reader doesn't have to follow your recommendations of course. Reviews are less formal than a report.

How to use this book

The main section of this book focuses on each task type individually, explaining its characteristics and providing guidance how to plan a response to an example question. For each task-type question, two responses from different candidates are provided. One response is very good and the other is less good, identifying areas that the candidate could improve on. There are detailed comments on each response, and a breakdown of the marks that the response could get in the exam. You should read these responses and commentary before you write your own response to the question. When you have written your response, look back at the comments and the mark scheme, and think about what you did well and also how you could have done better.

Preparing for the exam

It is important that you plan your time in the exam. You will need to complete both tasks within the 80 minutes. It is sensible to divide your time equally between the two tasks: about 40 minutes each. You should make sure that you:

- **Read** all of the questions carefully to be certain you understand what they mean.
- **Plan** your writing.
- **Write** your response according to your plan.
- **Check** your writing for errors.

Read the questions

Read the Part 1 question carefully, and identify the two given points to include and think about what your third point could be. Read all of the Part 2 questions. There will be three questions, and you will need to choose one. When making your choice, you will need to think about the task type, the topic and the language that you will need. For example, think about a question that asks for an article to be written about social media. If you know lots of nice vocabulary about social media, then this could be a good choice. Another question might require a report to be written about doing work experience and for recommendations. You may need to use modal verbs for this. If you aren't very sure about using modal verbs, this might not be a good question to answer.

It is good advice to spend time thinking about each question before you start writing. If you start one question and then realise that you don't feel confident about the ideas or language you need, you may need to change question.

Plan your writing

It is tempting to start writing as soon as you decide what question to answer, but spending some time planning is very sensible. Candidates plan their writing in different ways, but the following is an example of a plan for the essay question on page 6:

> <u>Intro:</u>   addicted to social media | use it every day | manage without? | no!
>
> <u>Para 1:</u> when younger | nagging mother | she didn't approve | generation gap | changed her mind
>
> <u>Para 2:</u> make friends on SM | keep in touch | would feel isolated | normal nowadays
>
> <u>Concl:</u>   try to take away my SM? | no!

Here, the candidate has noted down some ideas and good vocabulary to use, and has decided what will go in each paragraph.

Write your response

Use your notes to assemble your ideas from your plan into a well-organised piece of writing with a suitable tone and good, accurate language. With good planning technique, this will be easier. Of course, you will also be thinking about the functions, grammar and vocabulary that you considered before you started to produce your plan. This is the best way to make sure that you show the examiner as much of your language ability as possible.

It is a useful skill to paraphrase language that you find in the task. So, if the task says 'Could you live without social media?', you could answer by saying 'I couldn't live without social media.' But it would be better to paraphrase and say something like 'I'm quite sure I wouldn't be able to manage without my Facebook account!'

What language do you need?

There are three things to consider when you have read the questions. There is some overlap between them, but it is still a good idea to think about all three.

1. What functions does the task need?

For example, do you need to give your opinion, explain something or give a recommendation?

2. What grammar can you use in the task?

This may be linked to the functions of the question. For example, if you are asked to give a recommendation, you'll be able to use modal verbs (e.g. 'You should remember to…').

However, often the grammar you use will be your choice. If you know that you are confident when using conditional sentences, for example, can you include one in your response? If you know that you don't feel confident about using relative clauses, how can you avoid trying to use one?

3. What vocabulary is related to the task topic and links in with the functions?

If you are giving recommendations in the task, for instance maybe in a report, you should think about what phrases you can use to make sure that there is variety. For example, it is better not to start each idea with 'I think…'. You could use 'In my opinion…' or 'My view is…' as alternatives to make sure that you show the examiner a good range of different phrases. Other vocabulary that you decide to use will be related to the topic. If the task is about social media, for example, what vocabulary (e.g. *online, download, browse, click, followers*, etc.) might be good to use?

You can also think about which words or phrases you want to use to link ideas together. Using linking devices (e.g. *and, but, however, on the other hand, as opposed to*, etc.) helps with the organisation of your writing and makes it easier for the reader to understand it.

Check your writing

You should always leave five minutes to read through each response you write. Check that you haven't left anything important out, but also check the language for errors. For example:

Have you used the right tenses? Are there any spelling errors?

It's a good idea to make your own checklist while you prepare for the B2 First Writing paper. It will help you to think about what to check for, and also to think about mistakes that you know you often can make.

Here is a suggested checklist to use, but it's a good idea to add things that you know you sometimes make mistakes with.

What would you add to this checklist?

✔	✘	
☐		Does your response cover all of the content points in the task?
☐		Is your response in the right style for the task type?
☐		Have you used the right register for the task?
☐		Have you used paragraphs to separate different ideas?
☐		Have you used linking devices correctly?
☐		Have you got a range of linking devices?
☐		Are all tenses correct?
☐		Have you used articles with nouns where needed?
☐		Are the prepositions correct?
☐		What about errors you've made in the past?

The assessment criteria

Each piece of writing is marked against four assessment criteria, each carrying a maximum of five marks.

Content

This criterion focuses on whether you have answered the question and whether the reader would have all the information they need. You must make sure that you identify what the question is asking you to do and plan your answer so that you stay on the topic. In Part 1 there are three content points that you must cover: two that are given and one that you must add. In Part 2 questions you must identify what you will need to write about from the question.

Max. 5 marks

Communicative achievement

This criterion focuses on how well you communicate with the reader. This includes whether your writing is suitable for the task you are writing and that it also involves register. Register means whether your writing is more formal (e.g. writing for someone you don't know) or less formal (e.g. writing for your classmates).

Max. 5 marks

Organisation

This criterion focuses on how your ideas are organised into paragraphs, if these are needed. It includes the use of discourse markers (e.g. *and*, *but*, *so* at a basic level; and *therefore*, *despite this* at a higher level). It also includes things like how pronouns are used to refer to nouns to avoid repetition. For example: 'He never liked school and hated going there.' In this sentence, using the word 'there' means that the student doesn't repeat the word 'school'.

Max. 5 marks

Language

This criterion focuses on vocabulary and grammar. It isn't just about using vocabulary and grammar without making mistakes. It also considers whether your writing uses more difficult grammar and more unusual words and phrases. It is sometimes hard to focus on both, and, of course, it's great if you don't make any mistakes! However, if this means that your language is very simple, it may mean that you can't get to the top marks here.

Max. 5 marks

When all four criteria have been assessed your total mark is given out of 20.

B2 Writing | Cambridge Masterclass

Planning Guide

Write the question you are going to answer below, and underline or highlight the important words that will help you to focus your response.

What functions does the task need?

What grammar could you use?

What vocabulary could you use?

Bring your ideas together in a plan, and think about the organisation and register you need.

- How many paragraphs do you need? How will you link ideas?
- Who is your reader? What is your relationship to them?
- Do you need to use more formal or more informal language?

Plan:

Text type 1: Essay

B2 First Writing

In Part 1 of the Writing paper you will have to write an essay. **Remember:**

- You must answer this question.
- The topic will be something general, and you won't need expert knowledge.
- The reader will be your teacher – try to imagine them reading this.
- You must include the two points given in the notes and add your own idea.

Look at the following question. **Think about:**

- your own experience about what you would like to study
- good words related to technology that you could include
- what your own idea could be. You must include this to complete the task, and it needs to be different from the two points given.

In your English class you have been talking about education. Now your English teacher has asked you to write an essay.

Write an essay using **all** your notes and giving reasons for your point of view.

> Do schools need to make changes so that education is more suitable for young people?
>
> Write about:
>
> 1. Subjects
> 2. Use of technology
> 3. ………………………… (your own idea)

Read the following sample answers and see how two students have answered this task.

Student Response A

There is no doubt than some schools are stuck in the past. They aren't teaching in a way that is relevant to young people these days. Of course, others have moved with the times and are better.

Some subjects are taught in a very old fashioned way. I am thinking particularly of maths. Nowadays, we all have not only calculators at our fingertips, but also computers. Some think that we don't need to learn maths in the way our parents did as we can make better use of our time. Of course, understanding basic maths is important but what about adapting the maths to make it more relevant? For example, learning about how to manage personal finances and how to build spreadsheets for that.

This brings me to my second point, that teaching us how to use technology is better. We can learn a lot using technology.

Lastly, I wonder if we even need school buildings. We can learn from our homes with the internet. Maybe we could even change the hours that we study to allow students to choose the time that suits them best.

This is a good opening paragraph. It is short but it makes it clear that the student has understood the question.

The student uses a good structure here (not only... but also) to show an additional point.

The use of the rhetorical question here contributes to the communication of the essay well.

This paragraph is very short, and covers the second point in the notes but doesn't say much.

The student has actually added two extra points of their own in this final paragraph. This is fine, but remember that you have to add one to complete the task.

Text type 1: Essay

Content

Although both of the content points are included and a third idea is added, the essay in uneven as the first point is covered much better than the other two. However, they are all addressed, so the student still scores full marks for this criterion.

5 / 5

Communicative achievement

The tone is appropriate for an essay. Ideas are expressed logically and clearly which helps the student to communicate with the reader. This helps to make the essay interesting to read. The fact that the last two points are very brief means the reader would most likely want to know more about these and so this doesn't quite reach full marks here. More information on these might have held the reader's attention more.

4 / 5

Organisation

The ideas in the essay are well organised, and it is easy to follow the content of the essay. Paragraph 3 is very short and this stands out. The student has used good phrases to link ideas and to introduce paragraphs (e.g. 'This brings me to my second point…'). This links ideas across paragraphs clearly.

4 / 5

Language

The language used is suitable for giving opinions and providing examples. The student shows a good range of grammatical structures and vocabulary. For example, relative clauses: '…in a way that is relevant…'; passive form: 'Some subjects are taught…'. The student has very good control of language and is usually very accurate.

4 / 5

Total marks: 17 / 20

This is a good answer the question. The content is uneven in that the first point is given more space in the answer than the other two, but the reader would still be fully informed. The student has used a lot of good language, and the writing is very accurate. The essay is well organised, and it is easy to follow the ideas. Changes in ideas are well signalled, and the tone is appropriate.

Student Response B

I think education is very important and it must think carful about make change. Is not possible to change everything. But education must be change to be good for the youngs.

For example, I don't like sience and I don't like study it. Maybe we can to choose the subjects we like to study. Is better that we enjoy.

I very much like to study technology though. I would like to have this subject at school. It can be include play games maybe! That skill help me to be handy.

My idea is that the *horas* of the school be change. It always start very early as as a teen we don't like to get up early. We are youngs and we like to sleep later. This can be a change for education.

Weighing up all the arguments, the subjects, the technology and the horas should be change.

There is a paragraph for each idea in the essay, even though they are all short.

Be careful to check your writing for words that are similar in your language. Here the student has used the word for 'hours' in their own language.

This is a good phrase to use to conclude an essay, but here the student could have used it to bring all of their ideas together better. For example, they could have summarised the points they made about the subjects and the technology rather than just listing the three things to change.

The essay is only just above the required length. This is acceptable, but the student could have added to the essay to expand on some of their ideas. It is a good idea to recognise how much of a page is taken up by 140–190 words in your writing as this will mean that you don't need to count words in the exam.

Content

The essay is relevant to the topic in the question, and the student has covered the two points in the notes and they have added their own idea. They have slightly misunderstood the second idea as the notes refer to how technology is used, but the student thinks it is about studying technology as a subject. The added idea is logical and is linked to the topic.

4 / 5

Communicative achievement

The tone of the essay is not always consistent. In Paragraph 3 the use of the exclamation mark stands out: 'It can be include play games maybe!' The use of a personal example is relevant and helps to engage the reader with the content (e.g. 'For example, I don't like sience…'). The ideas are quite simple and are only just enough for B2 Level.

3 / 5

Organisation

The paragraphing is clear and there is a function for each one. The essay overall is quite short so there is less opportunity to use linking devices. In general, the linking devices are quite simple and some sentences could have been linked better (e.g. 'I very much like to study technology though **so** I would like to have this subject at school').

3 / 5

Language

All of the content can be understood, and the student makes their ideas known. There are a lot of errors though, which sometimes means that the reader has to stop reading in order to check meaning. The grammar used is simple, but it often isn't totally accurate. The student doesn't show good control of language.

2 / 5

Total marks: 12 / 20

The student has answered the question, which is good. There is some organisation, but this could be better and the tone used in the essay is slightly inconsistent. The language is the biggest problem for the student here. They have ideas to write about, but they haven't been able to show control of language at this level. The vocabulary is rather basic too, and so this is the area that is the weakest for this student.

B2 Writing | Cambridge Masterclass

Now have a go at writing a response to this question yourself.

In your English class you have been talking about education. Now your English teacher has asked you to write an essay.

Write an essay using **all** your notes and giving reasons for your point of view.

> Do schools need to make changes so that education is more suitable for young people?
>
> Write about:
>
> 1. Subjects
> 2. Use of technology
> 3. ………………………… (your own idea)

Highlight or underline the important words.

Outline plan:

Refer to the Planning Guide on page 12 for guidance on how to plan your response.

Write your response (140–190 words).

- [ ] Does your response cover all of the content points in the task?
- [ ] Is your response in the right style for the task type?
- [ ] Have you used the right register for the task?
- [ ] Have you used paragraphs to separate different ideas?
- [ ] Have you used linking devices correctly?
- [ ] Have you got a range of linking devices?
- [ ] Are all tenses correct?
- [ ] Have you used articles with nouns where needed?
- [ ] Are the prepositions correct?
- [ ] What about errors you've made in the past?

B2 First Writing

Text type 2: Article

In Part 2 of the Writing paper you may have the option of writing an article. **Remember:**

- An article is usually written for an English-language website, newspaper or magazine.
- A heading will help to catch your readers' attention.
- Try to make your article engaging and interesting to read.
- Try to have a strong ending to leave the reader with something to think about.

Look at the following question. **Think about:**

- who will read your article
- what functions you will be using, and what grammar and vocabulary these need
- how you will plan your paragraphs.

You see this announcement in an English-language magazine for young people:

> **COULD YOU LIVE WITHOUT SOCIAL MEDIA?**
>
> Could you imagine living without Facebook or Twitter?
> Is it possible?
>
> Would it be a good thing to do?
>
> Tell us why social media is important to you.
>
> Write an article for our magazine! We will publish the best articles next month.

Write your **article**.

Read the following sample answers and see how two students have answered this task.

Student Response A

No Social Media? Impossible!

I can admit. I am totally addicted to social media. I use it every day. Could I manage without it? I don't think so.

I can remember when I was younger and I was nagging my mother each day to allow to have a Facebook page. She didn't like it and didn't approve of social media at all. But I guess that's the generation gap! But after what seemed like years, eventually something changed her mind.

Whatever it was, I was overjoyed. I have made new friends on social media, and now keep in touch with old friends who I don't see in the flesh any more. If I hadn't made my social media pages, I am sure I would feel isolated now. It's normal for everyone to talk on social media and at difficult times, it has helped me to know I am not alone.

So, what will happen if you take my social media away? Really, you don't want to know! Try to living without it yourself to see.

This is a relevant title to the article; it ensures that the reader will know what the article is about.

The article starts with several very short sentences – a great opening to the article, and it catches the reader's attention.

This reference links back to the previous paragraph, and helps with the organisation of the paragraphs in general.

There is good movement between tenses in the sentences.

Possibly the last sentence here isn't needed, but it is still a strong ending and addresses the topic of the article well.

Text type 2: Article

Content

All content is relevant to the task. The student's article addresses the topic well and talks about different aspects of social media, including saying that they think social media is vital for them and how they use it, and clearly stating that they think they couldn't live without it. The reader would be fully informed.

5 / 5

Communicative achievement

The tone is suitable for an article. There is a good title that attracts the attention of readers. The start and the end of the article are particularly effective. The tone is consistent throughout and communicates with the reader well.

4 / 5

Organisation

There are suitable paragraphs in the article, and the student uses linking devices well. Some of the linking devices are more basic (e.g. 'and'; 'but'). Sometimes the use of linking devices is more ambitious though. The writer uses pronouns to indicate nouns well, which helps the text to be cohesive.

4 / 5

Language

Structures and vocabulary are generally used accurately. There is some excellent vocabulary (e.g. 'nagging'; 'overjoyed'; 'generation gap'; 'isolated'), and this is often used very accurately. There is some accurate collocation too (e.g. 'totally addicted'; 'manage without'; 'changed her mind'). There are a few mistakes, but these are often made with more difficult language (e.g. 'to allow to have a Facebook page' and 'try to living without It'), and there is also a lot of grammar that is accurate.

5 / 5

Total marks: 18 / 20

This is a very good article. It includes everything needed, and the language used is very strong. The student has thought about which language is appropriate for the task, and has included some excellent vocabulary. The style the student has used is suitable, and the target reader (the reader of the article) would be informed.

Student Response B

Is it impossible to survive these days without using social media?

In my opinion, I think is not possibal to be without social media in our times. However, I think is not very nice and we can miss some things without social media. Without social media we can't be knowing what is happen in the world. Social media is very important and it helps all to be friends. The people who start social media really don't know how important it is to survive this days.

On the other hand, you don't have to got social media and you can chose to not have it. It is your choice! Maybe if you are without your phone you will have more time to do other things. You can go to talk to your friends and drink a coffee with them. Sometimes its a good idea to put down your phone or your computer and leave it at home.

In conclution I think there are both sides to the arguement and you must make up your own mind on it You can use your phone all the time and forget your friends or you can leave it at your house and your home.

Moreover, you can save some money if you without phone. You don't have to pay for some time and then you can use this money to pay for something other. It's a good idea!

The student has used a heading, but it is mostly language taken from the question so they have missed the opportunity to demonstrate their language ability.

Spelling is only one part of Language, and students can still get good marks with some spelling mistakes in more complex words. However, the student should have been able to spell this word, as 'impossible' is in the question.

The discourse markers that the student uses are more suitable in essays (In my opinion; on the other hand; In conclusion; moreover). This makes the article feel more formal.

The article starts on topic and is relevant to the question. However, in the second part it moves away slightly and talks about using phones more than using social media.

The article is rather long (234 words). Try to keep to a maximum of 190 words, and make sure that you leave time to check your writing carefully for errors in language.

Text type 2: Article

Content

At the start of the article the content is relevant to the topic, but the second half goes off topic and the student writes more about the use of phones and other electronic devices. Remember to keep your answer on topic, and don't write about something similar that you have written about before.

3 / 5

Communicative achievement

The tone of review is not suitable for an article. The student has used some phrases that are more suitable to an essay, and the article feels more like an 'advantages and disadvantages' essay. This stops it engaging the reader and communicating ideas clearly.

2 / 5

Organisation

There are paragraphs but sometimes the order of the paragraphs doesn't seem right, particularly in the second part of the article. The discourse markers used are more suitable to essays, and there are different ways of linking ideas in articles. However, generally the text has organisation and makes use of some linking devices.

3 / 5

Language

Some of the phrases the student uses are taken from the question. Remember that it is better to paraphrase and use your own words. Some errors in the text are basic, such as missing subjects (e.g. 'I think is not very nice') and incorrect tenses (e.g. 'we can't be knowing'). Other language is accurate but quite simple. Occasionally, the language is very simple (e.g. 'However, I think is not very nice and we can miss some things without social media.').

3 / 5

Total marks: 11 / 20

This student has written an article that could have been improved. Some of the language has been taken straight from the question, and there are some errors. However, none of the errors stop the content being understood. The communicative achievement is the main weakness here as the student has written this more like an essay and so it is harder to imagine readers being interested in it.

B2 Writing | Cambridge Masterclass

Now have a go at writing a response to this question yourself.

You see this announcement in an English-language magazine for young people:

> **COULD YOU LIVE WITHOUT SOCIAL MEDIA?**
>
> Could you imagine living without Facebook or Twitter?
> Is it possible?
> Would it be a good thing to do?
> Tell us why social media is important to you.
> Write an article for our magazine! We will publish the best articles next month.

Write your **article**.

Highlight or underline the important words.

Outline plan:

Refer to the Planning Guide on page 12 for guidance on how to plan your response.

Text type 2: Article

Write your response (140–190 words).

✔	✘	
☐		Does your response cover all of the content points in the task?
☐		Is your response in the right style for the task type?
☐		Have you used the right register for the task?
☐		Have you used paragraphs to separate different ideas?
☐		Have you used linking devices correctly?
☐		Have you got a range of linking devices?
☐		Are all tenses correct?
☐		Have you used articles with nouns where needed?
☐		Are the prepositions correct?
☐		What about errors you've made in the past?

Text type 3: Email

B2 First Writing

In Part 2 of the Writing paper you may have the option of writing an email. **Remember:**

- You will be writing to someone you know.
- The email will be informal.
- You will have certain content to include.
- You can ask the person who has emailed questions too.

Look at the following question. **Think about:**

- how to cover the point about a gift
- what to say to your friend about your schedule.
- how you will plan the organisation of your email.

You have received this email from your English-speaking friend:

From: Jack
Subject: My visit

I'm so excited about coming to stay with you and am thinking about what to bring. I'd like to bring you something special from my country – name it! What would you like?

I know you will be at college some of the time but I hope we will be able to do some things together. Will you have some free time?

I think I can get the bus from the airport to your house. My flight arrives very early in the morning and the buses start early too.

Jack

Write your **email**.

Read the following sample answers and see how two students have answered this task.

Student Response A

Hi Jack,

I'm so pleased you are looking forward to coming to Manchester. It's a great city and there is lots to do. You may need another holiday when you get home. I have lots of things for us to do.

I am hoping that I will have finished all of my courses at college when you get here so don't worry about being left alone. If I haven't finished them, it won't be a problem as my brother will look after you. He really wants to take you to watch Manchester United play football if he can get tickets. I know that will excite you!

Don't worry about getting the bus from the airport. With all your bags it will be better if I come and pick you up. I have a car now so it will be easy. Don't forget to text me your flight information though.

You really don't need to bring me anything. What? You insist on it? Okay! Well, you remember how I loved that honey that is made locally. I'd love a small jar of that!

Don't forget those flight information!

Chris

This is a very friendly, welcoming opening to the email and sets a suitable tone for the email.

The start of this complex sentence shows two different tenses used very accurately.

This is the second multi-part verb (also known as a phrasal verb) in the email, and shows good use of vocabulary.

The student has made a mistake here. You don't have to write in perfect English to get full marks, but maybe if they had checked their work more carefully they would have spotted this basic error.

The email is well organised with a suitable opening and close, and this final sentence reminding the friend of something is a good way to finish an email.

Content

The email is very clear and covers all of the points mentioned in the task. The reader would be fully informed as the student has given lots of information. The response is near the top of the word limit, but it is very thorough. They have covered the points in a different order to the question email, but this doesn't matter.

5 / 5

Communicative achievement

The email is consistent in its tone throughout and has the right register. It is friendly and there is also humour in it which helps to make the email easy to read and for the reader to imagine the friendly relationship between the student and their friend. It communicates very well and is natural.

5 / 5

Organisation

The organisation of the email is excellent. The student uses paragraphs to separate the different ideas, and different grammatical structures to link ideas. There aren't many individual linking words, but these aren't needed due to the use of grammar (e.g. I am hoping that I will have finished all of my courses at college when you get here so don't worry about being left alone.). Three 'ideas' are included in the one sentence very naturally.

5 / 5

Language

The student has excellent control of language. They have demonstrated that they know a lot of grammar (e.g. different tenses, conditional sentences, relative clauses) as well as some good vocabulary. The email is very accurate in addition to having this wide range of language.

5 / 5

Total marks: 20 / 20

This student is at the top of the level for this test. Their writing is fluent and natural. The target reader, their friend, would understand everything in the email, and the tone and effect of the language used is very positive. The writing is well organised and clear.

Student Response B

Dear my friend.

Please come at my home for vist. Thanks for sending me your address. I'm so excited about coming to stay with you and am thinking about what to bring. I will to bring some clothses and my other things. I will be exciting to visit with you. I think is raining in there. So I must to brougth too a umbbrerella wich is very necesarry

I'd like to bring you something special from my country – name it! It's name is a nice sweet dish name is 'cheesecake'. I think you like it very mush.

My bus. It arrives early in the morning so I can come. to your house very quick. Please dont forget me! I will bring mush bags so. I have a car now so it will be easy. I come to you with my car.

Kisses from your frined

Sara

Here and in other places in the email, the student has used full stops incorrectly. A full stop indicates the end of a sentence, and these errors make the email hard to read.

This is taken from the text. The student hasn't understood it, but it is important to paraphrase any information you use from the task. This means putting the words in the text into different words.

This spelling error possibly comes from a problem with pronunciation of this word.

This phrase doesn't fit well with the communication of the email, and the reader might not understand what the student means.

Content

The student has misunderstood the task, and, although they refer to some of the points in the task, these references wouldn't be clear to the reader. They have copied some chunks of language from the task, and this would be a problem for the target reader who would be confused about who was travelling. The email is short and is just over the bottom word limit of 140 words.

2 / 5

Communicative achievement

The reader of this email would be confused. The information included is not logical considering the content of the task. The reader would not have all the information they need from this email so communication is poor. However, the student has attempted to use a suitable tone.

2 / 5

Organisation

There is an attempt at organisation, and the student has used paragraphs. However, there are frequent full stops in the middle of sentences that make the email difficult to read. The linking devices that are used correctly are usually in language taken from the question. The student does not show a good understanding of how to link ideas.

2 / 5

Language

The student doesn't have good control of language. The only parts of the email that are accurate are taken from the task. Some of the errors are basic, such as errors in tenses (e.g. 'I will to bring'), and there are many spelling errors and many of these are made with basic words (e.g. 'clothese'; 'mush'; 'brought').

2 / 5

Total marks: 8 / 20

This student response is below the level required for this test. They have attempted to reply to the email but haven't really understand the content well enough. They don't show sufficient language ability, either in grammar or vocabulary, to complete the task to the level required.

Now have a go at writing a response to this question yourself.

You have received this email from your English-speaking friend:

> **From:** Jack
> **Subject:** My visit
>
> I'm so excited about coming to stay with you and am thinking about what to bring. I'd like to bring you something special from my country – name it! What would you like?
>
> I know you will be at college some of the time but I hope we will be able to do some things together. Will you have some free time?
>
> I think I can get the bus from the airport to your house. My flight arrives very early in the morning and the buses start early too.
>
> Jack

Write your **email**.

Highlight or underline the important words.

Outline plan:

Refer to the Planning Guide on page 12 for guidance on how to plan your response.

Text type 3: Email

Write your response (140–190 words).

B2 Writing | Cambridge Masterclass

✓ ✗

- [ ] Does your response cover all of the content points in the task?
- [ ] Is your response in the right style for the task type?
- [ ] Have you used the right register for the task?
- [ ] Have you used paragraphs to separate different ideas?
- [ ] Have you used linking devices correctly?
- [ ] Have you got a range of linking devices?
- [ ] Are all tenses correct?
- [ ] Have you used articles with nouns where needed?
- [ ] Are the prepositions correct?
- [ ] What about errors you've made in the past?

B2 First Writing

Text type 4: Letter of application

In Part 2 of the Writing paper you may have the option of writing a letter of application.

Remember:

- The question will tell you who you are writing to.
- You need a suitable opening and close for the letter.
- The register of letter will be quite formal.
- You don't have to tell the truth about yourself.

Look at the following question. Think about:

- the sort of people the café owner expects to apply for the job
- the skills the café owner will expect the writer to have
- how to make your application attractive.

You see this notice on an English-language website:

ARE YOU LOOKING FOR A PART-TIME JOB?

Our small café is in a tourist area and we are looking for temporary part-time staff this summer. Would you like to work in our kitchen helping our chef, or work serving customers?

Email me telling me which role you would like and why you would be suitable. Good English is essential for waiting staff.

Apply to Mrs Thompson by 30th June.

Write your **letter of application**.

Read the following sample answers and see how two students have answered this task.

Student Response A

Dear Mrs Thompson,

I am very interested the notice which was posted on the Eurostudy website and would like to apply for a job in your café.

I believe I am suited to either of the roles mentioned. My English is good and last year I passed my English diploma with top grades so I would be happy talking to tourists visiting from different countries in English. However, I would be most interested in working in the kitchen as I am enrolled at catering college which starts after the summer. I love cooking and one day I plan to become a chef. I hope I could learn from the chef as well as earning some money before my course commences.

I am hard-working, punctual and am keen to learn. I hope to receive a positive response to my application. I look forward to hearing from you at your earliest convenience.

Stephanie Chambers

This is a clear opening and says straight away why the student is writing the letter.

The tone throughout the letter is very polite, and this would impress the owner of the café.

This is excellent vocabulary. The student has shown that they know a more difficult word than 'starts'.

This is likely to be a whole phrase that the student has learned. It can be useful to learn phrases like these, but make sure that you use them in appropriate situations. This is used well here.

Usually we would end a letter with a closing salutation, like 'Yours sincerely' or 'Kind regards'. This is missing, but it doesn't have a big impact on the letter. The student closes with their full name.

Text type 4: Letter of application

Content

All content is fully relevant to the task. The owner of the café would have a very clear idea of what job the student is interested in, and would be able to judge if they are suitable.

5 / 5

Communicative achievement

The register is semi-formal, which is appropriate for a job application. There is a polite tone throughout the letter and the owner of the café would be able to see from the content what skills the student has. They have communicated very clearly.

5 / 5

Organisation

The letter is well structured with short opening and closing paragraphs. The main paragraph includes the important information about the student's job preference and their reasons for applying for the job. The student uses some linking devices, such as 'However' and ' so', but they also use structure and language to link ideas (e.g. 'I would be happy talking to tourists visiting from…') which helps to organise ideas.

5 / 5

Language

The language used is extremely accurate. The student has very good control of structures and has been able to show some high-level vocabulary (e.g. 'catering'; 'commences'). While there isn't a lot of complex grammar, it is all suitable for the task and is used well.

5 / 5

Total marks: 20 / 20

This letter has been written by a very confident student who has really understood what the task required. The tone of the letter holds the reader's attention, and ideas are clearly communicated with accurate language that is quite complex. The student has full control of the language they use. Although the letter is only 141 words long, at the lower end of the word range, it is concise and completes the task well.

Student Response B

Hello!

My name is Fabio and I have see your notice! I am very excite to know that I can work in you café maybe.

I think I can work in the kitchen as I am a very good cooker. I work for many years in a big restaurant in my country.

I very much work in many different country and can know the different cuisine.

I can start work on 1st July and finish work on the summer end. I ask you to tell to me how much the money will be for one day?

My friends tell to me that I am very expert and they all eat my cook and love it.

Please email me on fabiogram@abc.com

Your friend,

Fabio

Although you may start a letter to someone you know like this, here the student needs to be more formal.

The student uses an exclamation mark here, and again later in the letter – this isn't appropriate for a letter applying for a job.

This a common mistake, and there are a number of mistakes with words in this letter.

This is a good word, but it seems a little out of place here when the rest of the language used in very informal.

The letter has a lot of paragraphs. The student could have combined some sentences to make a paragraph with a clearer function.

Text type 4: Letter of application

Content

The student has covered all of the elements of the task: the reader would know that they want a job, which job they want and why they think they would be suitable. Although there are issues with other areas of the letter, the content is all included.

5 / 5

Communicative achievement

The letter does not communicate well. The owner of the café would be expecting a more formal letter suitable for a job application. The opening and close of the letter are more suitable for when writing to a friend. This would not give a good impression. However, the tone is consistent throughout.

2 / 5

Organisation

The student uses a new paragraph for almost all sentences. The letter isn't very well organised, and it feels as if it is unplanned. Some similar ideas could have been placed together in one paragraph (e.g. the 2nd, 3rd and 5th paragraphs). The linking devices the student uses are quite simple.

2 / 5

Language

The student is able to use language to communicate their ideas, but there is a lack of accuracy. Some of the errors are basic, such as 'I have see' and 'I am very excite'. The errors don't stop the reader understanding the meaning. The range of language is very limited. If the student had shown a wider range, despite the errors, they might have got 3 marks here.

2 / 5

Total marks: 11 / 20

This student has included all of the information needed to complete the task, and it is all relevant. However, the other areas are not as strong. Like the Student A response, the answer is quite short at 142 words. This answer isn't well organised, and the student could have used more words to link ideas together more effectively. The reader might be confused by the tone. The number of paragraphs and lack of linking devices doesn't help to make it easy to read the letter.

Now have a go at writing a response to this question yourself.

You see this notice on an English-language website:

> **ARE YOU LOOKING FOR A PART-TIME JOB?**
>
> Our small café is in a tourist area and we are looking for temporary part-time staff this summer. Would you like to work in our kitchen helping our chef, or work serving customers?
>
> Email me telling me which role you would like and why you would be suitable. Good English is essential for waiting staff.
>
> Apply to Mrs Thompson by 30th June.

Write your **letter of application**.

Highlight or underline the important words.

Outline plan:

Refer to the Planning Guide on page 12 for guidance on how to plan your response.

Text type 4: Letter of application

Write your response (140–190 words).

B2 Writing | Cambridge Masterclass

☑ ☒

☐ Does your response cover all of the content points in the task?

☐ Is your response in the right style for the task type?

☐ Have you used the right register for the task?

☐ Have you used paragraphs to separate different ideas?

☐ Have you used linking devices correctly?

☐ Have you got a range of linking devices?

☐ Are all tenses correct?

☐ Have you used articles with nouns where needed?

☐ Are the prepositions correct?

☐ What about errors you've made in the past?

B2 First Writing

Text type 5: Report

In Part 2 of the Writing paper you may have the option of writing a report.

Remember:

- A report gives facts but you can also give your opinion.
- You need to consider who will be reading your report.
- Sometimes the structures needed in a report will be fairly simple.
- Using headings may help you to plan your report.

Look at the following question.

Think about:

- the register you should use to write a report for your school principal
- the vocabulary relating to work that you know
- the different parts of the work experience you want to comment on.

You recently took part in a work-experience programme organised by your college when you spent some time in a local company.

Your school principal has asked you to write a report about your experience.

You should give your opinion about:

- whether you enjoyed the work experience
- what the company asked you do to during the work experience
- how the programme could be improved.

Write your **report**.

Read the following sample answers and see how two students have answered this task.

47

Student Response A

Report on work experience

The work experience programme I participated in last month was a valuable experience. I had been looking forward to it all year and my expectations weren't disappointed.

The heading here isn't exciting, but, unlike headings in articles, it doesn't need to be. Reports are more factual.

Before I started the experience I was given all the necessary information and this showed good organisation by the college. It is a very important thing to give full, detailed information to all students. However, the name of the person I needed to call was not given.

This is excellent paraphrasing. The student has used a different phrase to the one used in the question, but it shows the same meaning.

During the two weeks of the work experience, I helped in the company which allowed me to follow some of the important office procedures, including replying to the emails from customers. I learnt a lot from this about the correct way to write to important people.

In this report the student has integrated their suggestions into the main part of the text. Student B takes a different approach – both are fine.

When I returned to college, to business course, I wanted to be able to compare my experience to other students' experience but there wasn't time before our exams started. I suggest that the work experience is not so late in the school year to make time for this.

The tone of the report is appropriate. The language is fairly formal, and the effect is that it communicates appropriately with the school principal.

Overall, it was a very positive two weeks and I highly recommend it to future students.

This answer is slightly over length at 219 words. The student should have tried to keep within the word limit.

Content

All content is fully relevant to the task. Although the report is a little long, it is very good writing so this wouldn't be a problem. The report gives relevant information about the work experience and includes suggestions for improvements.

5 / 5

Communicative achievement

The register is semi-formal which is appropriate for communicating with the college principal. The student is polite in their criticism of some things related to the programme, and nobody would be offended. The tone is fully appropriate, and the reader could find this easy to follow.

4 / 5

Organisation

The report has a simple but clear heading that states what it is about. Reports can use sub-headings, but this isn't essential. The organisation here is clear and the student has planned their work well with each paragraph having a good focus. They have used structures well to link ideas within sentences (e.g. in paragraph 3: 'I helped in the company which allowed me…' – the relative clause here helps with internal cohesion.

4 / 5

Language

The student has demonstrated that they have a good control of grammar. This includes the past perfect tense (e.g. 'I had been looking forward'), the passive form (e.g. 'I was given') and reduced relative clauses (e.g. 'the name of the person I needed to call'). The student has thought about how they can show their language ability. On the whole, the vocabulary is not complex, but it is entirely suitable for the task. With some more complex vocabulary, this could have been given 5 marks.

4 / 5

Total marks: 17 / 20

The student has produced a report that fully informs the reader as all content is relevant and the points in the question are all covered. The tone is suitable for a report as it is semi-formal. The ideas are well organised, and language is generally very accurate.

Student Response B

INTRODUCTION

I recently took part in a work-experience programme organised by your college and I think it was very good. It is a good idea and I had a good time.

ORGANSIATION

The company organised the work experience very well and I had all that I needed before I went to the college which was very good.

DAILY TASKS

During the first week I did very easy tasks in the company and sometimes I felt very bored. Despite this, in the second week I could see that the reason I did those tasks. I saw the value of the tasks. I conclude the tasks were very good. I think more tasks can be very useful too.

RECCOMENDATIONS

In my opinion, next year the students could listen to the experience of the student's this year to get a better experience in the college. This experience will help with them to know what is going to happen.

CONCULTION

The work experience is a very good idea and the college was very good to do it. In my opinion is very useful. Well done!

The use of headings for each section of the report helps to organise it into logical sections.

In the first paragraph alone the student has used the same words a number of times. Try to use a variety of words, even if they mean the same thing, to show the examiner that you have a wide vocabulary.

The student repeats the same noun a lot in this part of the report. If they had used a pronoun as a substitute, this would have read better (e.g. *I conclude that ~~the tasks~~ they were very good.*).

Generally, the tone of the report is consistent and is semi-formal. This is suitable for a report. However, the report ends with 'Well done!' which is not consistent.

Text type 5: Report

Content

Although the student starts well, there is some confusion about where the work experience has taken place further on in the report. The student has confused the words 'company' and 'college', and the principal of the college may be slightly confused by this. Apart from this, the student talks about their experience, says what they enjoyed and makes a suggestion for improving the programme.

4 / 5

Communicative achievement

The tone is generally appropriate for a report. The language is in a semi-formal register, and, with the exception of the ending, is consistent. The layout is suitable for a report, and so it does communicate to the reader – but the ideas are quite simple. The repetition of some words makes the report less effective at communicating clearly (e.g. the word 'experience is used three times in the Recommendations paragraph).

3 / 5

Organisation

Reports can have a main heading and sub-headings. This isn't the only way to organise reports, but it is useful to include these and the student has used sub-headings to help to define each paragraph. However, the short sentences and the use of basic linking words make the report more difficult to read.

3 / 5

Language

In general, apart from the confusion between company and college, the student has communicated their ideas but there are a lot of errors. There is a lack of variety in the language, and this limits the marks that the student can be awarded. Instead of using the word 'good' so many times, the student could have used other words to show that they have a better vocabulary (e.g. 'It is ~~a good~~ an excellent idea'; or change the wording to show a different structure: '~~…and I had a good time.~~ I found it very informative').

3 / 5

Total marks: 14 / 20

The student has included all of the content that was asked for in the question, so the reader would be fully informed. The ideas are all quite simple, and in certain places there is a little bit of confusion with some of the word choices. The repetition of the same words in the report means that the student hasn't shown a good range of vocabulary. The organisation overall could have been better, and this would have lifted the mark.

B2 Writing | Cambridge Masterclass

Now have a go at writing a response to this question yourself.

You recently took part in a work-experience programme organised by your college when you spent some time in a local company.

Your school principal has asked you to write a report about your experience.

You should give your opinion about:

- whether you enjoyed the work experience
- what the company asked you do to during the work experience
- how the programme could be improved.

Write your **report**.

Highlight or underline the important words.

Outline plan:

Refer to the Planning Guide on page 12 for guidance on how to plan your response.

Text type 5: Report

Write your response (140–190 words).

B2 Writing | Cambridge Masterclass

_____
_____
_____
_____
_____
_____
_____
_____
_____
_____
_____
_____
_____
_____
_____

✔ ✘

- [ ] Does your response cover all of the content points in the task?
- [ ] Is your response in the right style for the task type?
- [ ] Have you used the right register for the task?
- [ ] Have you used paragraphs to separate different ideas?
- [ ] Have you used linking devices correctly?
- [ ] Have you got a range of linking devices?
- [ ] Are all tenses correct?
- [ ] Have you used articles with nouns where needed?
- [ ] Are the prepositions correct?
- [ ] What about errors you've made in the past?

Text type 6: Review

B2 First Writing

In Part 2 of the Writing paper you may have the option of writing a review.

Remember:

- A review is usually written for an English Language website, newspaper or magazine.
- You will need to give your opinion on something – it can be positive, negative or mixed.
- You will need to use language to describe things and explain your opinion.
- Usually, a review ends with a conclusion about your overall opinion.

Look at the following question. **Think about:**

- who will read your review
- how you will structure the review
- what impressive vocabulary you could use.

You see this announcement on an English-language website:

REVIEWS WANTED!

Have you used an app to help you learn English?

Write a review for our website telling us why you decided to use the app, how you think it has helped you with learning English, and whether you would recommend it to other language learners.

We will post the best reviews on our website

Write your **review**.

Read the following sample answers and see how two students have answered this task.

Student Response A

LOVE LANGUAGE APP!

If you love learning English, then you are sure to love the Love Language App! I was fed up of wasting my time on my bus journey each day and when I found this app I was convinced it was the best way for me to make use of my travel time.

The thing I like most about it is the part where you have to listen to sentences and repeat them. It's a big help for pronunciation which as I'm sure you know, is very confusing in English. This app has really helped me. If you want to improve your speaking then I highly recomend you to get this app.

Like anything, it isn't perfect but I think it is exceptional value for money and your teacher will be impressed when your speaking gets more fluent. In my opinion, you won't regret using your time on your journey to school each day doing extra studying.

Strong opening with a conditional sentence that catches the reader's attention.

Good use of phrasal verb.

Clear paragraphing with one paragraph for each point in the question.

Although this is not spelled correctly, this is a minor error and does not stop the reader from understanding the meaning. Remember that the text doesn't have to be perfect to get very good marks.

The use of the phrase 'in my opinion' is suitable here as the student sums up their feelings about the app.

Text type 6: Review

Content

All content is relevant to the task. The review covers the three points mentioned in the question: why they started using the app (because they wanted to use the time they spent travelling), how it has helped with their language learning (it has helped their pronunciation) and whether they would recommend it (yes – it's good value).

5 / 5

Communicative achievement

The student starts the review with a title that clearly shows what the review is about, and an opening sentence that communicates well. This holds the reader's attention. The tone of the review is effective, and makes the reader want to read the review.

5 / 5

Organisation

The review is well organised, and it is coherent. It is clearly paragraphed, and each paragraph has a logical purpose. There is some use of linking devices, but this could have been more ambitious (e.g. these two sentences: 'The thing I like most about it is the part where you have to listen to sentences and repeat them.' and 'It's a big help for pronunciation which as I'm sure you know, is very confusing in English.' could have been joined with a relative clause. This would have made the paragraph flow better and would have shown the examiner some more grammar.).

4 / 5

Language

There is a range of vocabulary and also structures. The student uses more ambitious language (e.g. 'I was convinced' rather than 'I knew'; and 'I was fed up with…' rather than 'I didn't like…'). Structures and vocabulary are generally used very accurately. Some of the sentences are complex and have many clauses.

5 / 5

Total marks: 19 / 20

This review is very strong, and the student has thought about the functions they need to include to write a convincing review. They have explained and justified their opinion well. It communicates effectively with the target reader, and it would hold their attention. There is an ambitious range of language that is used very well.

Student Response B

Are you looking for an app to learn English? Well I was looking and I thought I have found the perfect app to use on my phone. It was very easy to download and I was so happy to find that it was free! That's great news for us students wich don't have much money. I can imagine you know this situation, can't you? I wanted to learn much more vocabulary as that is the most difficult for me. The app has lots of different topics and you can read a new word and then hear how is it said. I love it as I can remember so many new vocabulary. After you studied a group of words there is a little test. I liked to check if I can remember the words and usually I can! Then, do I recommend the app. I can! It's a great app but there are lots of advertisments. I find those quiet annoying. But then, on the other hand it's free! So you can make up your mind! Download it soon and you can make your English much better.

Using a question to get someone's attention is a good idea.

The student uses the past continuous tense here accurately, but then, instead of using the past perfect in the second part of the sentence, makes a mistake and uses the present perfect.

The student has made an attempt to use 'after' as a way of linking the two ideas in this sentence.

The student has included information on two out of the three points mentioned in the question, but they haven't said why they started using the app. It is important to include all of the points to make sure that you can achieve full marks.

Text type 6: Review

Content

The content is relevant to the task, but the student doesn't include information on why they started using the app. The rest of the content is appropriate to the task, but the target reader wouldn't be fully informed by this.

3 / 5

Communicative achievement

The tone of review is suitable and engaging. The reader would be interested in reading the review, and would feel that they are going to learn about the language-learning app.

4 / 5

Organisation

The student has written their response in one paragraph, and this makes the review more difficult to read. There aren't many attempts to use more ambitious linking devices (e.g. they mostly use 'and' and 'but'). However, they do use the adverb 'after' in the middle of the review. This was the weakest part of the student's response and maybe if they had thought more about the organisation while they were planning, this could have been better.

2 / 5

Language

There are attempts at a range of structure, part-continuous tense, relative clause, modal verbs and question tags. However, there are quite a lot of errors. There is a mix of some control of more simple structures and a lack of control of more ambitious structures. There is some good vocabulary (e.g. 'on the other hand'; 'make up your mind'). There are some spelling errors, but these don't stop the reader understanding the review.

3 / 5

Total marks: 12 / 20

This review is more difficult to read than the Student A response. The organisation is lacking, and there are several errors in language. The tone is good though, and the student communicates well with the target reader. The student hasn't checked that they have included all of the required content though, so the reader wouldn't be fully informed.

B2 Writing | Cambridge Masterclass

Now have a go at writing a response to this question yourself.

You see this announcement on an English-language website:

> **REVIEWS WANTED!**
>
> Have you used an app to help you learn English?
>
> Write a review for our website telling us why you decided to use the app, how you think it has helped you with learning English, and whether you would recommend it to other language learners.
>
> We will post the best reviews on our website.

Write your **review**.

Highlight or underline the important words.

Outline plan:

Refer to the Planning Guide on page 12 for guidance on how to plan your response.

Write your response (140–190 words).

✓	✗	
☐		Does your response cover all of the content points in the task?
☐		Is your response in the right style for the task type?
☐		Have you used the right register for the task?
☐		Have you used paragraphs to separate different ideas?
☐		Have you used linking devices correctly?
☐		Have you got a range of linking devices?
☐		Are all tenses correct?
☐		Have you used articles with nouns where needed?
☐		Are the prepositions correct?
☐		What about errors you've made in the past?

Practice tests

Test 1 | p.65

Question	Topic	Task type
1	Sport	essay
2	Cooking	article
3	Gardening	letter
4	Art gallery visit	report

Test 2 | p.75

Question	Topic	Task type
1	Town v country	essay
2	Office help	letter
3	Wearable device	review
4	Money	article

Test 3 | p.85

Question	Topic	Task type
1	Environment	essay
2	Trip to stay with family	letter
3	Olympics	review
4	Funny film	article

Test 4 | p.95

Question	Topic	Task type
1	Work	essay
2	Gyms	review
3	Travel	article
4	Winning a prize	email

Cambridge B2 First Writing

Practice test 1

Planning page

Part 1

You must answer this question. Write your answer in 140–190 words in an appropriate style on the separate answer sheet.

1   In your English class you have been talking about sport. Now your English teacher has asked you to write an essay.

   Write an essay using **all** your notes and giving reasons for your point of view.

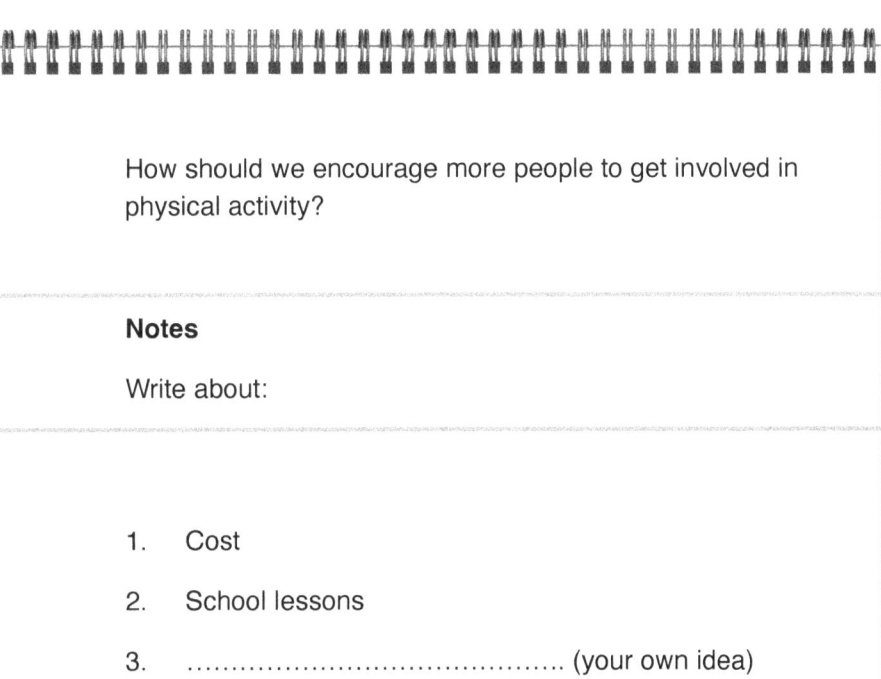

How should we encourage more people to get involved in physical activity?

Notes

Write about:

1. Cost
2. School lessons
3. ………………………………….. (your own idea)

Answer sheet page 1

Part One Answer
Write within the lines.

Answer sheet page 2

Part One Answer
Write within the lines.

Planning page

Part 2

Write an answer to one of the questions 2–4 in this part. Write your answer in 140–190 words in an appropriate style on the separate answer sheet.

2   You see this announcement in an English-language magazine:

> **LOVE OR HATE COOKING?**
>
> Next month we will feature food and cooking in our magazine. How did you learn to cook? Who taught you? Do you enjoy it? Tell us all about it!
>
> Write an article for our magazine! We will publish the best articles next month.

Write your **article**.

3   You see this notice on an English-language website:

> **Gardening help needed!**
>
> I need help for a few hours a week from someone who knows about gardening and plants. Write me a letter telling me what experience you have and when you are available to work. I don't live near a bus route so you must be able to get to Albury yourself.
>
> Mr Jenkins

Write your **letter of application**.

4   Your college organised a visit to an art gallery recently. Now your college principal has asked you to write a report about your experience saying whether you think it would be a good place to visit again. You should give your opinion about:

- whether you enjoyed the visit
- how the visit helped your studies
- the organisation of the visit.

Write your **report**.

Answer sheet page 1

Part Two Answer
Write within the lines.

Answer sheet page 2

Part Two Answer
Write within the lines.

Cambridge B2 First Writing

Practice test 2

Planning page

Part 1

You must answer this question. Write your answer in 140–190 words in an appropriate style on the separate answer sheet.

1. In your English class you have been talking about places to live. Now your English teacher has asked you to write an essay.

    Write an essay using **all** your notes and giving reasons for your point of view.

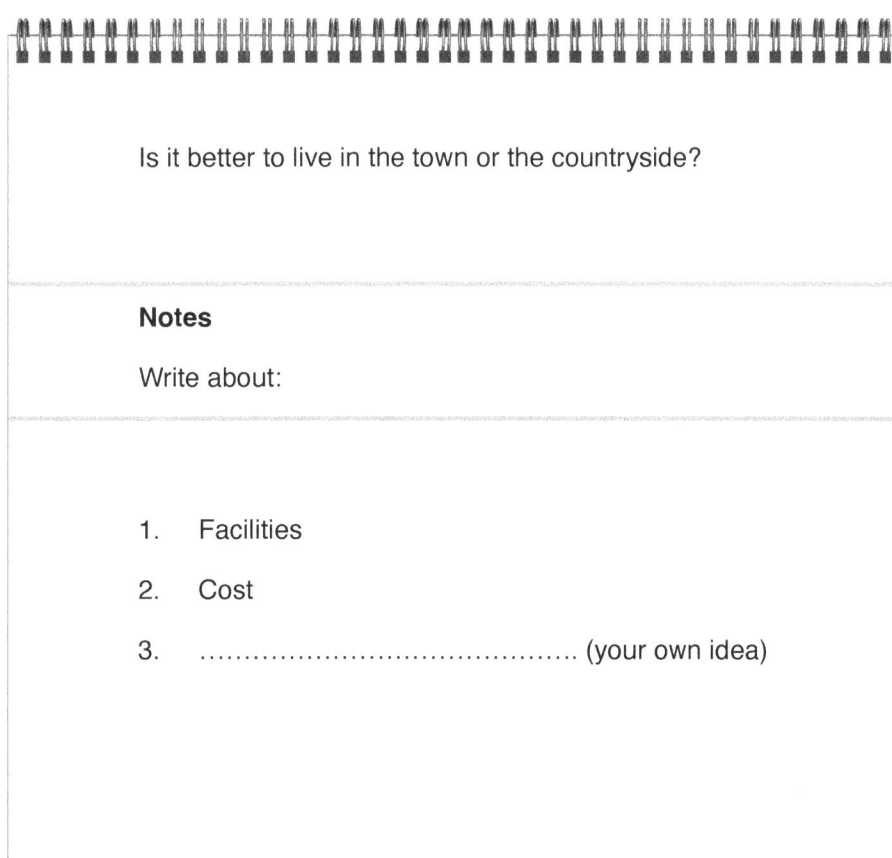

Is it better to live in the town or the countryside?

Notes

Write about:

1. Facilities
2. Cost
3. ………………………………….. (your own idea)

Answer sheet page 1

Part One Answer
Write within the lines.

Answer sheet page 2

Part One Answer
Write within the lines.

Planning page

Part 2

Write an answer to one of the questions 2–4 in this part. Write your answer in 140–190 words in an appropriate style on the separate answer sheet.

2   You see this announcement on your college website:

> ### OFFICE HELP
> We are looking for a student to help in our college office for a few hours a week while we are really busy at the start of the year. We need someone who is organised and good at talking to people. Apply in writing to Mrs Benson. Please include details of any relevant experience and tell us when you would be available to work.

   Write your **letter of application**.

3   You see this announcement on an English-language website:

> ### REVIEWS WANTED!
> Have you recently bought a device you can wear to track your activity, like a smart watch that counts your steps? We are featuring these wearable devices next month and are looking for reviews to include:
>
> - What is the best feature of your wearable device?
> - How much did is cost and was it worth it?
> - What can't your device do that would be useful?
>
> We will include the best reviews on our website next month.

   Write your **review**.

4   You see this announcement in an English-language magazine:

> ### MONEY!
> Are you good or bad at managing your money? Do you always know how much money you have or do you always run out? We are looking for articles for next month's magazine. Write an article for our magazine telling us your experience and how you think young people should be taught to manage their money! We will publish the best articles next month.

   Write your **report**.

Answer sheet page 1

Part Two Answer
Write within the lines.

Answer sheet page 2

Part Two Answer
Write within the lines.

Cambridge B2 First Writing

Practice test 3

Planning page

Part 1

You must answer this question. Write your answer in 140–190 words in an appropriate style on the separate answer sheet.

1   In your English class you have been talking about the environment. Now your English teacher has asked you to write an essay.

Write an essay using **all** your notes and giving reasons for your point of view.

What can people do to help the environment?

Notes

Write about:

1. Recycling
2. Transport
3. ………………………………….. (your own idea)

Answer sheet page 1

Part One Answer
Write within the lines.

Answer sheet page 2

Part One Answer
Write within the lines.

Planning page

Part 2

Write an answer to one of the questions 2–4 in this part. Write your answer in 140–190 words in an appropriate style on the separate answer sheet.

2   Your college is organising a trip where you can go and stay with a family in an English-speaking country. You went on a similar trip last year and now the college principal has asked you to write a report saying:

- how the trip helped you to practice your English
- what you did on the trip
- how the trip could be improved.

Write your **report**.

3   You have received this email from your English-speaking friend:

> Help!
>
> I have a school project to do about the Olympics and I wondered if you could help me. I remember you went to the games when they were held in your country, didn't you? What did you watch? I think you said it was expensive, but was it worth it? What was the best thing for you?
>
> Can you email back and let me know?

Write your **email**.

4   You see this announcement in an English-language magazine:

> **REVIEWS WANTED!**
>
> Have you recently seen a film that really made you laugh?
> We are looking for reviews of funny films for our website. Tell us the name of the film, why it was funny and whether you would recommend it.
>
> We will post the best reviews on our website.

Write your **review**.

Answer sheet page 1

Part Two Answer
Write within the lines.

Answer sheet page 2

Part Two Answer
Write within the lines.

Cambridge B2 First Writing

Practice test 4

Planning page

Part 1

You must answer this question. Write your answer in 140–190 words in an appropriate style on the separate answer sheet.

1   In your English class you have been talking about work and jobs. Now your English teacher has asked you to write an essay.

Write an essay using **all** your notes and giving reasons for your point of view.

What is the most important thing to consider when thinking about a future career?

Notes

Write about:

1. Pay
2. Job security
3. ………………………………….. (your own idea)

Answer sheet page 1

Part One Answer
Write within the lines.

Answer sheet page 2

Part One Answer
Write within the lines.

Planning page

Part 2

Write an answer to one of the questions 2–4 in this part. Write your answer in 140–190 words in an appropriate style on the separate answer sheet.

---

2   You see this announcement on an English-language website:

GYM REVIEWS

Have you joined a gym to get fit recently? We are looking for reviews of local gyms to put on our website. Write us a review giving information about the facilities, the cost and saying whether you would recommend it.

We will post the best reviews on our website.

Write your **review**.

3   You see this announcement in an English-language magazine:

TRAVEL

Travel is our feature topic next month and we would like to know about your opinions.
Is it better to travel with someone or to travel alone? Why would you choose to travel this way?
Tell us about your experiences in an article for our magazine!
We will publish the best articles next month.

Write your **article**.

4   You have received this email from your English-speaking friend:

Great news!
I've won a prize from our local shopping centre. I get a voucher for lunch there for two people, as well as tickets for the cinema. Do you want to come with me? I want to try that new pizza place but I have no idea what films are good now. Do you?
I need to tell them when we want to go so that they can book for us.
When are you free? Let me know. I'm so excited!

Write your **email**.

Answer sheet page 1

Part Two Answer
Write within the lines.

Answer sheet page 2

Part Two Answer
Write within the lines.

Find more Cambridge English exam-practice resources at www.prosperityeducation.net

www.ingramcontent.com/pod-product-compliance
Lightning Source LLC
Chambersburg PA
CBHW051317110526
44590CB00031B/4382